Data Ethics & Privacy in AI

Using Data Without Violating Human Rights

By Joe Correa

Published by Live Stronger Faster

This book is for educational and informational purposes only. The author and publisher are not engaged in rendering legal, financial, or other professional advice. Readers should consult a qualified professional before making any financial decisions.

First Edition

Table of Contents

Overview

Artificial intelligence does not begin with algorithms. It begins with data. Every prediction, every automated decision, every recommendation, and every risk score generated by an AI system is built on one foundational ingredient: human information. Names, faces, voices, financial records, health histories, browsing behavior, location data, biometric identifiers, and even emotional signals are captured, processed, and transformed into digital representations of real people. In the age of AI, data is not just a technical input—it is a form of power over human lives. Whoever controls data controls what machines learn, how people are judged, and who receives opportunity or harm. That is why data ethics has become one of the most urgent moral, legal, and political questions of the modern era.

For decades, companies treated data as a corporate asset rather than a human right. Information was harvested quietly, stored indefinitely, sold to third parties, and repurposed far beyond its original intent. This model worked when data was used for basic analytics and advertising, but it becomes dangerous when that same data fuels autonomous decision-making systems that determine who gets a loan, who gets a job, who receives medical treatment, who is flagged as suspicious, or who is denied access to services. AI has turned data from a passive record into an active force. It shapes futures. It creates winners and losers. It embeds the past into the future. Without strong ethical rules, this power becomes a form of invisible governance that operates without public consent or democratic oversight.

The explosion of AI has also exposed a fundamental contradiction in the digital economy. On one hand, data is more valuable than oil, driving trillion-dollar industries and national competitiveness. On the other hand, that same data represents the most intimate details of human existence. Health conditions, mental health struggles, family relationships, genetic profiles, financial hardship, and private communications are now routinely processed by machines at massive scale. When AI systems ingest this data, they do not merely store it—they analyze, predict, infer, and often create new information about people that they never consented to reveal. The ethical question is no longer just "Who collected the data?" but "What does the machine now know about me, and who controls that knowledge?"

This tension is why governments around the world have moved to regulate data more aggressively than ever before. Laws such as Europe's General Data Protection Regulation (GDPR), California's Consumer Privacy Act (CCPA), Brazil's

LGPD, and healthcare protections like HIPAA were designed for a pre-AI world, yet they now serve as the legal foundation for controlling AI behavior. These laws assert that individuals have rights over their data, including the right to access it, correct it, delete it, restrict its use, and know how it is being processed. In an AI context, these rights become exponentially more important—and far more difficult to enforce. How do you delete data that has already been used to train a model? How do you explain a decision made by a neural network trained on millions of private records? How do you withdraw consent from a system that has learned from you?

The challenge is that AI does not just use data—it transforms it. Once personal information is used to train a machine learning model, it becomes embedded in statistical patterns, latent variables, and predictive structures that cannot simply be erased. Even if the original record is deleted, its influence remains. This creates a new ethical and legal frontier: the right to be forgotten in a world where machines never truly forget. Regulators are now grappling with whether models themselves can become illegal if they were trained on unlawfully obtained data, and whether organizations must retrain or destroy models when consent is withdrawn. The financial, legal, and operational implications of this shift are enormous, and they are only beginning to be understood. At the same time, corporations have built entire business models around what scholars now call “surveillance capitalism”—the practice of collecting vast amounts of behavioral data in order to predict, influence, and monetize human behavior. AI supercharges this system by turning raw surveillance into real-time psychological targeting, dynamic pricing, risk scoring, and automated persuasion. In this environment, privacy is no longer just about secrecy; it is about autonomy. When machines know what you are likely to do, believe, or buy before you do, the line between free choice and algorithmic manipulation begins to blur. Data ethics is therefore not just about protecting information—it is about protecting human agency in a world of predictive machines.

Healthcare data provides one of the clearest examples of what is at stake. AI systems are increasingly used to analyze medical records, genetic data, imaging scans, wearable device signals, and even voice patterns to predict disease, personalize treatment, and manage populations. The benefits are extraordinary, but so are the risks. A data breach in healthcare can expose not just credit card numbers, but cancer diagnoses, fertility treatments, mental health conditions, and genetic vulnerabilities. Even worse, when this data is used to train AI models, it can create systems that silently discriminate, deny care, or misclassify patients based on biased or incomplete datasets. HIPAA was designed to protect medical records, but it was never designed to regulate AI models trained on millions of them.

Financial data is equally sensitive and equally powerful. AI-driven credit scoring, fraud detection, underwriting, and risk management systems rely on deep pools of transaction data, employment histories, debt records, and behavioral signals. These systems can dramatically expand access to credit—but they can also create new forms of digital redlining, financial exclusion, and opaque discrimination. When data ethics fails in finance, people do not just lose privacy—they lose homes, businesses, and futures. Regulators now increasingly view algorithmic financial decisions as subject to the same fair lending and consumer protection laws as human decision-makers, forcing banks and fintech companies to rethink how data is collected, processed, and governed.

Children's data presents one of the most ethically fraught areas of all. AI-powered educational platforms, games, social networks, and monitoring tools collect enormous volumes of information about minors, often without meaningful consent. This data can follow a child for life, shaping how they are profiled, targeted, and judged as adults. Laws such as COPPA and GDPR's child protections recognize that children cannot meaningfully consent in the same way adults can, yet AI systems increasingly learn from them anyway. The ethical question is not simply whether this data is legal to collect, but whether it is moral to build lifelong digital profiles before a person even understands what privacy means.

As data breaches become more frequent and more severe, the ethical failures of AI data governance become impossible to ignore. When a traditional database is hacked, records are stolen. When an AI system is compromised, models, training data, and inferred attributes can be exposed or manipulated, creating cascading risks across entire populations. The cost of these failures is not just financial; it is social and political. Trust in digital systems collapses when people believe their data is unsafe or abused. In a world increasingly governed by AI, that loss of trust can destabilize entire economies and institutions.

To address these challenges, new approaches to privacy-preserving AI are emerging. Techniques such as differential privacy, federated learning, homomorphic encryption, and secure enclaves aim to allow machines to learn from data without exposing or centralizing it. Synthetic data seeks to replace real personal information with statistically similar but artificial datasets. These tools offer hope that AI can be powerful without being invasive—but they also introduce new risks, tradeoffs, and governance questions. Ethical AI is no longer just about whether data is collected, but how it is transformed, protected, and mathematically constrained.

This book exists because data ethics is now the frontline of AI governance. Every lawsuit, regulatory fine, public scandal, and government crackdown on AI begins with data. Who collected it. How it was used. Whether consent was real. Whether privacy was respected. Whether harm occurred. Organizations that treat data as a free resource will find themselves facing legal, financial, and reputational disaster. Those that treat data as a form of human dignity will earn trust, loyalty, and long-term legitimacy in an AI-driven world.

In the chapters that follow, you will explore who truly owns data in the age of AI, how consent must be designed, how surveillance capitalism operates, how sensitive domains like health, finance, and children's data require special protection, how breaches create systemic risk, and how privacy-preserving technologies can reshape the future of AI. You will also confront one of the most radical ideas of modern digital law: the right to be forgotten, and whether it can survive in a world where machines never stop learning. Data ethics is not a technical footnote—it is the moral foundation of every intelligent system. Without it, AI becomes not just powerful, but dangerous.

Chapter 1

Who Owns Data in the AI Universe

The question of who owns data sits at the center of every ethical and legal conflict surrounding artificial intelligence. In the physical world, ownership is straightforward: if you buy a house, a car, or a piece of land, it belongs to you. In the digital world, however, ownership becomes ambiguous the moment information is copied, transmitted, and transformed. A medical record can exist in a hospital database, a cloud server, an insurance company's archive, and an AI training dataset all at the same time. Unlike physical property, data can be duplicated endlessly without leaving the original holder. Yet even when it is copied, the data still represents a real human being. That human carries the consequences of how the data is used, even if they no longer control it.

Historically, companies have treated data as something they own simply because they collected it. When a user clicks "I agree," corporations interpret that moment as a transfer of rights. In practice, this means that an individual's behavior, preferences, and personal attributes become corporate assets that can be sold, analyzed, or combined with other datasets for profit. Artificial intelligence amplifies this imbalance because the value of data increases exponentially when it is used to train predictive models. A single person's data may seem insignificant, but when millions of people's data are combined, the resulting AI system can influence markets, politics, healthcare, and entire populations.

Modern privacy law challenges this assumption by asserting that people do not give up ownership of their data simply because it was collected. Under frameworks such as GDPR and CCPA, individuals are recognized as the true owners of their personal information, while companies are merely custodians or processors. This means organizations have a duty to protect, justify, and limit how they use data. AI complicates this structure because machine learning systems create new forms of data derived from the original—predictions, scores, classifications, and inferred traits. These derived data points often reveal more about a person than the raw data itself, yet they are rarely treated as something the individual has rights over.

For example, a bank may collect income and payment history, but an AI model might infer that a person is financially unstable, likely to default, or at risk of bankruptcy. That inference becomes part of how the person is treated, even though they never consented to that conclusion being created. The model's output can affect loan approvals, interest rates, and access to credit, yet the individual cannot easily see, correct, or challenge it. In this sense, AI does not just use data—it creates new digital identities that exist beyond human control.

Ownership becomes even more complex when data is sold, shared, or licensed. Data brokers aggregate information from hundreds of sources and sell profiles to advertisers, insurers, and political campaigns. AI companies buy or scrape massive datasets from the internet, including images, voices, social media posts, and written content, often without explicit permission. The people behind that data may never know their information was used to train a machine that now competes with them, profiles them, or monetizes their identity. The law struggles to keep pace with this reality because traditional ownership concepts were never designed for a world where machines learn from human experience.

Another major issue is that AI models trained on personal data effectively internalize that information. Even if a company deletes the original records, the model may still contain traces of that data in its learned patterns. This raises the question of whether individuals own not just their raw data, but also the models trained on it. Courts and regulators are beginning to consider whether a model trained on illegally obtained or improperly consented data is itself unlawful. If the answer is yes, entire AI systems may need to be destroyed or retrained, creating massive financial and operational consequences.

Governments are increasingly pushing toward the idea that people have ongoing rights over their data, even after it has been used. This includes the right to know how their data is processed, the right to object to certain uses, and the right to demand deletion. For AI, this means organizations must track where data comes from, how it flows through systems, and how it influences automated decisions. Data ownership is no longer a philosophical question—it is becoming a compliance requirement.

True ethical AI begins with recognizing that data is not just a resource, but a representation of human lives. When companies treat data as property they own, they reduce people to inputs. When they treat data as something borrowed under conditions of trust, they are forced to design systems that respect dignity, autonomy, and fairness. Ownership, in this sense, is about power: who gets to decide how information is used, who benefits from it, and who bears the risk when something goes wrong.

As AI continues to expand into healthcare, finance, education, and government, the stakes of data ownership will only grow. Whoever controls the data controls the narrative of who people are, what they deserve, and what they are allowed to do. Ethical AI demands that this power remain anchored to the individuals whose lives are being turned into data in the first place.

The Woman Inside the Algorithm

Maya first realized something was wrong when her mortgage application was denied in less than three seconds. She had a steady job, a strong credit score, and enough savings for a down payment, yet the screen simply flashed “Application Rejected – Risk Profile Not Approved.” There was no explanation, no appeal button, no human contact. Just a decision made by a system she could not see. When she called the bank, the representative sounded confused. “The system says you’re high risk,” he said. “I’m not sure why. The model doesn’t tell us.”

Maya spent weeks digging into her own life, trying to find the invisible flaw that had turned her into a liability. She pulled her credit reports, reviewed her medical history, and checked every financial transaction she could find. Everything looked normal. Yet somewhere, inside an AI system she had never met, a version of her existed that was apparently dangerous. That digital Maya—constructed from years of data, transactions, online activity, and third-party records—had become more powerful than the real one.

Eventually, she discovered that a data broker had sold a profile linking her address to someone else's bankruptcy, and an insurance algorithm had inferred that she was at risk of long-term illness based on anonymized health statistics from her neighborhood. None of it was true, but the AI didn't know that. It only knew probabilities. Those probabilities had hardened into facts inside the machine, and those facts were now governing her future.

Maya tried to correct the errors, but every company pointed to another system. The bank blamed the model. The model provider blamed the data. The data broker said it only sold what it had. No one could tell her how to delete the false version of herself that now lived inside dozens of algorithms. She realized she didn't own her digital identity anymore. It had been sold, copied, and learned by machines that would never forget.

One night, she imagined all the versions of herself scattered across servers around the world—each one whispering a slightly different story about who she was. Some versions said she was risky. Others said she was fragile. Others said she was not worth the investment. None of them were her, yet all of them had power over her life.

Maya finally found a small privacy advocacy group that helped her file data access and deletion requests under new AI transparency laws. It took months, but slowly, pieces of the false profile began to disappear. Models were retrained. Records were corrected. Decisions were reversed. When she was finally approved for her mortgage, she cried—not because of the house, but because she had reclaimed a piece of herself from the machines.

Standing in her empty living room, Maya realized something that would never leave her. In the age of artificial intelligence, your data is your shadow. If you do not own it, something else will. And that something will decide who you are allowed to become.

Chapter 2

Consent & Collection When it Comes to AI Decision Making

Consent is the moral and legal gateway through which all ethical data collection must pass. Without consent, data becomes extraction rather than participation. In the age of artificial intelligence, this distinction has become more important than ever because data is no longer used for a single purpose—it is used to create machines that continue learning long after the original interaction has ended. When a person gives consent to share their information, they are rarely agreeing to become part of a permanent training dataset that may be used, sold, or repurposed for decades. Yet that is exactly what happens in most AI systems today.

Traditional consent models were designed for a simpler digital world. A user clicked a box to allow a website to store cookies, or a patient signed a form allowing a hospital to access medical records. Those actions were tied to specific, limited uses. AI breaks that model because machine learning systems transform data into generalized knowledge that can be applied far beyond the original context. When you give a health app permission to track your heart rate, you are not just sharing numbers—you are contributing to a model that might predict disease, influence insurance pricing, or be sold to third parties for research. The original consent rarely reflects this expanded reality.

One of the greatest ethical failures in modern AI is the illusion of informed consent. People are shown long, technical privacy policies written by lawyers, not humans. They are told to accept or lose access to essential services. There is no meaningful negotiation, no real understanding of what will happen to their data, and no way to opt out of the most invasive uses. From an ethical perspective, consent obtained through complexity, coercion, or dependency is not true consent at all. It is compliance.

Regulators have begun to recognize this. Laws such as GDPR require consent to be informed, specific, freely given, and revocable. This means companies must explain what data they collect, why they collect it, how it will be used, and who it will be shared with. For AI, this creates a serious problem because many organizations cannot fully predict how data will be used once it enters a machine learning pipeline. Models evolve, new use cases emerge, and data may be reused for purposes that did not exist when it was collected. Ethical AI therefore requires dynamic consent–a system that allows people to continuously manage how their data is used as technology changes. Collection itself is another major ethical battleground. Modern AI systems thrive on scale, pushing companies to collect as much data as possible from as many sources as possible. This has led to the rise of ambient surveillance: phones tracking location, apps recording behavior, cameras analyzing faces, and platforms monitoring speech and emotion. Much of this collection happens without people realizing the full scope of what is being captured. In many cases, data is collected not because it is needed, but because it might be valuable someday. This "collect first, decide later" mindset is fundamentally incompatible with ethical governance.

In sensitive domains such as healthcare, finance, and children's data, consent and collection carry even higher stakes. A child cannot meaningfully agree to have their learning patterns analyzed for life. A patient in a medical crisis cannot negotiate how their genetic data will be used. A low-income borrower cannot freely refuse financial data sharing when it determines access to housing. Ethical AI must recognize these power imbalances and impose stricter rules where consent cannot be truly voluntary.

AI also enables indirect data collection—where information about a person is inferred rather than explicitly provided. A model can predict sexual orientation, political beliefs, mental health status, or pregnancy based on seemingly harmless signals. These inferences may be highly accurate, yet the individual never consented to having them created. From an ethical standpoint, inferred data should be treated as personal data, even if it was never directly collected. Otherwise, AI becomes a tool for extracting secrets people never agreed to share.

To build trustworthy AI, organizations must redesign how consent works. This includes plain-language explanations, real opt-out mechanisms, data minimization, and ongoing user control. Consent must become a living process, not a one-time click. Collection must be purposeful, limited, and accountable. Anything less turns AI into a system of quiet exploitation.

Ultimately, consent and collection define whether AI is a partnership with humanity or a form of digital colonization. When people control how their data enters machines, AI can serve them. When they do not, AI learns to serve those who extract the most from them. The ethical future of artificial intelligence depends on which model wins.

The Click That Never Ended

Daniel was just trying to check his blood pressure.

The health app on his phone had promised to help him stay alive. It asked him to agree to a new privacy update before it would open. He was standing in a pharmacy aisle, feeling dizzy, so he tapped "Accept" without reading. He did not know that in that moment, he had agreed to share not only his heart rate, but his sleep patterns, exercise habits, location data, and even the sound of his breathing with an AI analytics company halfway across the world.

Months later, Daniel was denied life insurance.

The letter said he was a high-risk applicant. He had no idea why. He was forty-two, exercised regularly, and had no major illnesses. When he requested an explanation, the insurer cited a predictive model trained on "biometric and behavioral health indicators." Those indicators had come from the very app he used to stay healthy.

Daniel learned that the app had sold anonymized data to an AI company, which had re-identified patterns and created a risk profile. His restless sleep, irregular work schedule, and elevated heart rate during stressful meetings had been interpreted as signs of long-term disease. He had never agreed to that. Or had he?

Buried in the privacy policy was a clause allowing "research and analytics use." That single phrase had given machines permission to learn everything about him.

Daniel tried to opt out, but the data had already been used. The model had learned. His digital self now existed in a thousand servers, predicting futures he had never chosen. A single click, made in a moment of weakness, had become permanent.

Standing in the pharmacy again months later, Daniel stared at the same app. He realized something terrifying. Consent, in the age of AI, was not a doorway. It was a one-way street. And he had walked down it without ever knowing where it led.

Chapter 3

Surveillance Capitalism in the New AI Economy

Surveillance capitalism is the economic engine that drives much of today's artificial intelligence. It is built on the idea that human behavior can be monitored, recorded, predicted, and monetized at scale. In this system, people are no longer simply customers; they become data sources whose lives generate raw material for machine learning systems. Every click, every movement, every message, every biometric signal becomes a data point in a massive behavioral marketplace. Artificial intelligence transforms this data into predictive products that are sold to advertisers, insurers, political campaigns, and governments, turning human experience into an extractive industry.

What makes surveillance capitalism uniquely dangerous in the age of AI is its asymmetry of power. Individuals generate the data, but corporations own the systems that analyze and profit from it. AI models can infer desires, fears, vulnerabilities, and future behavior with astonishing accuracy. These predictions allow organizations to nudge, manipulate, and influence people in ways that are largely invisible. The result is a form of economic control that operates without force, without direct coercion, and often without awareness. People believe they are making free choices, while algorithms quietly shape what options they see and which ones are pushed out of reach.

The rise of smart devices has dramatically expanded the reach of surveillance capitalism. Phones track location, watches monitor heart rate, cameras recognize faces, microphones listen for voice commands, and online platforms record every interaction. This creates a continuous stream of behavioral data that AI systems can analyze in real time. Unlike traditional market research, which relied on surveys and samples, AI-driven surveillance captures nearly everything. The world itself becomes a data collection machine.

This data is then used to build behavioral prediction engines. These engines do not just tell companies what people did; they tell them what people are likely to do next. In advertising, this means predicting what you will buy. In finance, it means predicting whether you will default. In politics, it means predicting how you will vote. In policing, it means predicting whether you will commit a crime. The more data AI systems collect, the more confident these predictions become—and the more power they wield over individuals and societies.

One of the greatest ethical problems with surveillance capitalism is that it erodes meaningful consent. Most people do not knowingly agree to be tracked across every app, website, and device they use. Even when consent is technically given, it is often buried in complex legal language or bundled with essential services that people cannot realistically refuse. AI systems thrive on this coerced data flow, learning more about people than those people ever intended to share.

Surveillance capitalism also creates new forms of inequality. Those with money, influence, or technical knowledge can shield themselves from tracking. Everyone else becomes transparent. Low-income communities, marginalized groups, and children are often the most heavily monitored, because they rely on free platforms, public services, and digital tools that monetize data. AI trained on this data can then reinforce existing inequalities by making decisions based on biased or incomplete information.

The psychological impact of constant monitoring is profound. When people know they are being watched, even by machines, they behave differently. They self-censor, conform, and avoid risks. AI-driven surveillance turns society into a digital panopticon, where control is maintained not by force, but by the expectation of being observed. This undermines creativity, dissent, and human freedom. Governments have begun to recognize the dangers of surveillance capitalism, especially when combined with AI. Data protection laws, algorithmic accountability rules, and bans on certain types of biometric surveillance are attempts to restore balance. But enforcement remains difficult when technology evolves faster than law.

To build ethical AI, societies must confront the business model itself. If AI is powered by the extraction of human behavior, then no amount of technical safeguards will fully protect privacy or autonomy. A future where AI serves humanity requires moving away from surveillance as the default and toward systems that respect boundaries, minimize data, and prioritize human dignity over profit.

The City That Watched Back

The cameras were everywhere, but people had stopped noticing.

Elena walked through her city every day surrounded by lenses—on streetlights, store entrances, apartment buildings, and transit stations. They were small, silent, and always on. Officially, they were there for safety. Unofficially, they fed the city's AI system, which predicted everything from traffic patterns to criminal behavior. Most people accepted it. The system made the city feel efficient, modern, and secure.

Until it decided Elena was a problem.

One morning, her subway pass stopped working. The screen flashed "Access Denied." At work, her building badge failed. Later, a loan she had applied for was mysteriously rejected. It was as if invisible doors were closing all around her. When she finally reached a human official, he hesitated before speaking. "The system flagged you as high risk," he said quietly. "Your behavioral profile suggests instability."

Elena demanded to know why. The answer was a web of data: late-night walks, a visit to a mental health clinic, messages she had sent about being exhausted and frustrated. None of it was illegal. None of it was dangerous. But the AI had learned that people who looked like her in the data often struggled financially or emotionally. And so it predicted that she would too.

She realized the city was not just watching her—it was deciding who she was allowed to be.

Every camera, every sensor, every algorithm had quietly turned her life into a forecast. And once a machine believes it knows your future, it starts shaping it.

Elena began to cover her face, leave her phone behind, and avoid monitored spaces. It felt like disappearing in plain sight. But she also felt something else: freedom. For the first time, she was not feeding the machine that had judged her.

Looking up at the blinking lenses, she whispered a promise to herself. “You can watch me,” she said. “But you will not own me.”

Chapter 4

The Intimacy of Health Data

Health data is the most intimate form of information a person can possess. It reveals not only who someone is today, but what their body may become tomorrow. Diagnoses, genetic markers, mental health records, fertility data, medication histories, biometric readings, and even patterns of movement and speech can now be captured, analyzed, and interpreted by artificial intelligence systems. In the age of AI, health data is no longer confined to hospital charts. It flows through wearable devices, mobile apps, insurance platforms, research databases, and machine-learning pipelines, creating a digital mirror of human biology that is both powerful and dangerously vulnerable.

AI promises extraordinary advances in medicine. Algorithms can detect cancer earlier than doctors, predict heart attacks, personalize treatments, and discover new drugs at unprecedented speed. These breakthroughs depend on vast quantities of patient data. Yet the same data that makes AI powerful also makes it perilous. When health information is misused, leaked, or misinterpreted, the harm is not abstract. It affects employment, insurance coverage, social standing, family relationships, and even personal safety. A single data point—such as a genetic risk factor or mental health diagnosis—can follow a person for life if it escapes into the wrong hands.

Historically, health privacy has been protected by strict legal frameworks such as HIPAA in the United States and medical confidentiality laws around the world. These rules were designed for a world where records were kept by doctors and hospitals. AI breaks this model because health data is now collected by technology companies that are not traditional healthcare providers. Fitness trackers, wellness apps, telehealth platforms, and AI symptom checkers gather sensitive information outside the boundaries of medical law. Much of this data is not covered by traditional protections, even though it is just as revealing as a doctor's chart.

AI also creates new forms of health data through inference. By analyzing patterns in behavior, speech, typing speed, facial expression, or movement, algorithms can predict depression, anxiety, neurodegenerative disease, pregnancy, or substance abuse. A person may never tell anyone these things, yet a machine can infer them with high accuracy. This inferred health data is often not treated as medical information under the law, even though it can be just as sensitive. The result is a vast shadow health record that exists beyond patient awareness or control. One of the most dangerous risks of

AI-driven health data is discrimination. Insurers, employers, and lenders have strong incentives to know whether someone is likely to become sick, disabled, or mentally unstable. Even when direct use of medical records is illegal, predictive models can be trained on health-related data to quietly exclude or penalize people. A model may not say "this person has cancer," but it may say "this person is high risk," which has the same effect. Ethical AI requires that health data, whether direct or inferred, be treated as protected and off-limits for harmful uses.

Data breaches in healthcare are uniquely catastrophic. Unlike credit card numbers, you cannot change your DNA or erase a diagnosis. When AI systems are trained on centralized medical databases, they become highly valuable targets for hackers, foreign governments, and criminals. A breach can expose millions of lives in ways that are irreversible. As AI systems grow more powerful, they must also become more secure, transparent, and accountable. Health data cannot be treated like any other dataset.

To protect patients in the AI era, new governance models are emerging. Privacy-preserving machine learning, secure data enclaves, federated learning, and synthetic data allow algorithms to learn from medical information without exposing or centralizing it. These technologies offer a way to advance medicine without sacrificing dignity. However, they require strong institutional commitment, regulatory enforcement, and ethical leadership. Without these, the pressure to maximize data and profit will always overwhelm privacy.

Ultimately, health data forces society to confront the deepest question of AI ethics: should machines be allowed to know our bodies better than we do? The answer will shape the future of medicine, insurance, employment, and human freedom. Ethical AI in healthcare is not about slowing innovation—it is about ensuring that progress does not come at the cost of human rights.

The Diagnosis She Never Gave

Lena found out she was sick from a marketing email.

The subject line read, "Support for Your Condition." She almost deleted it, assuming it was spam, until she saw the words "early-stage neurological disorder" in the preview text. Her heart raced. She had never been diagnosed with anything like that. She felt fine. Or at least she thought she did.

The email came from a wellness platform she had used for meditation and sleep tracking. Somewhere inside its AI system, her late-night restlessness, slowed typing, and slight changes in speech during voice journaling had been analyzed. The model had concluded that she was likely developing a degenerative condition. That prediction had been sold to an advertising network that targeted people with specific medical needs. Within days, ads for expensive treatments and experimental drugs followed her everywhere. Even her insurance company quietly adjusted her premiums.

Lena went to a doctor in a panic. After tests, he told her she was healthy. But the AI didn't care. The digital version of Lena was now labeled as sick. That label traveled faster than the truth.

She tried to erase it, but no one could tell her where it lived. The app said it only provided wellness insights. The ad company said it bought anonymized data. The insurers said they used predictive models, not diagnoses.

Standing in her kitchen, Lena realized that a machine had given her a diagnosis she never agreed to receive—and the world had believed it.

From that day on, she became cautious about every digital footprint she left. Her body was her own. But her data had been taken. And in the age of AI, that could be just as dangerous.

Chapter 5

Financial Data, the Bloodstream of Modern AI

Every transaction, loan application, paycheck, credit card purchase, mobile payment, investment decision, and digital wallet interaction generates information that reveals not only what a person owns, but how they live. AI systems are trained on this data to predict creditworthiness, spending behavior, fraud risk, insurance costs, investment profiles, and economic stability. Unlike most other categories of personal information, financial data directly determines a person's access to opportunity. When AI systems control how that data is interpreted, they effectively control who is allowed to participate in modern life.

In the pre-AI era, financial decisions were made by human underwriters, loan officers, and analysts. These people could make mistakes, but their reasoning was visible and could be challenged. AI replaces this with models that operate on millions of hidden variables. A person may be denied a mortgage not because of income or debt, but because their transaction history resembles that of someone else who defaulted. They may be charged a higher interest rate because their spending patterns resemble those of people who struggle financially. These correlations may be statistically valid but ethically devastating, because they convert probabilistic group behavior into personal judgment.

Financial data is uniquely dangerous because it creates feedback loops. When an AI system decides someone is high risk, it raises their costs, limits their access to credit, and increases their likelihood of financial stress. That stress then generates new data that confirms the model's original prediction. Over time, the algorithm becomes self-fulfilling. Entire communities can be algorithmically trapped in cycles of high interest, low investment, and restricted opportunity without a single explicit discriminatory rule ever being written.

Most people have no idea how much financial data about them exists. Banks, credit bureaus, payment processors, fintech apps, debt collectors, data brokers, and marketing platforms all collect, store, and trade financial behavior. AI systems combine this data into detailed economic profiles that predict not just what people have done, but what they will do next. This includes the likelihood of job loss, medical bankruptcy, divorce, or default. These predictions are sold as "risk analytics," but they often function as invisible gatekeepers that determine who gets access to housing, education, entrepreneurship, and wealth. Privacy laws have struggled to keep pace with this reality. While regulations protect account numbers and personal identifiers, they often do not protect behavioral financial data or algorithmic inferences. A person's credit score is regulated, but the AI model that predicts their long-term financial stability is often considered proprietary. This creates a legal loophole where companies can deny opportunity based on hidden predictions without accountability.

AI also introduces new risks of financial surveillance. Digital wallets, buy-now-pay-later apps, cryptocurrency platforms, and embedded finance systems allow companies to monitor spending in real time. This data can be used to adjust prices, limit access, or trigger interventions automatically. In authoritarian or unstable regimes, such systems can become tools of economic control. In corporate settings, they become tools of behavioral manipulation.

Ethical financial AI requires strict limits on how data is used. It must prohibit the use of financial data to infer sensitive traits such as health, religion, or political beliefs. It must require transparency when AI makes decisions that affect access to money. It must ensure that people can challenge, correct, and override algorithmic judgments. Most importantly, it must recognize that financial data is not just information—it is the digital representation of a person's ability to survive. When AI governs money, it governs freedom.

If financial data is abused, entire populations can be quietly excluded from prosperity. Ethical governance is not optional. It is the foundation of economic justice in the AI age.

The Account That Knew Too Much

When Marcus's debit card stopped working, he thought it was a glitch.

He stood in line at a grocery store with a cart full of food, embarrassed as the terminal beeped "Declined." He checked his balance on his phone. There was money there. Plenty of it. But the system refused the transaction. The clerk shrugged. "It happens sometimes," she said. Marcus left the store with nothing.

By the end of the week, his credit card limits had dropped. A loan he had pre-qualified for was suddenly unavailable. Even his rideshare app started asking for prepaid deposits before letting him book. It was as if the financial system had quietly turned against him.

When Marcus finally reached a customer service agent at his bank, the answer made no sense. "Our risk model has adjusted your financial profile," the woman said carefully. "Your transaction patterns indicate elevated future instability."

"What does that even mean?" Marcus asked.

It meant that the AI had noticed he had started buying cheaper groceries, had been late on a utility bill after his hours were cut, and had searched online for debt relief. The model concluded he was likely to struggle financially. That prediction had been shared across partner systems. Now every company saw him as a risk.

Marcus hadn't failed yet. But the machine had decided he would.

The harder he tried to stay afloat, the more the algorithm tightened around him. Higher interest rates. Lower limits. More restrictions. It was like being punished for a future that had not happened.

He realized something terrifying: the system didn't care if he proved it wrong. It was built to be right.

Standing outside the bank one night, Marcus looked at the glowing screens inside. His entire financial life lived there now, reduced to probabilities. And those probabilities were deciding whether he was allowed to survive.

In a world run by AI, money was no longer something you earned. It was something the machine allowed you to have.

Chapter 6

Children, AI, and the Data-Exposed Generation

Can you believe children are the most data-exposed generation in all of human history? From the moment a child is born, their life begins to generate digital records: hospital charts, biometric scans, baby monitor data, school profiles, learning platforms, social media traces, gaming activity, location histories, and behavioral analytics. Artificial intelligence systems ingest this information at scale, turning childhood into a lifelong data stream that begins before consent is even possible. Unlike adults, children cannot meaningfully understand or negotiate the terms under which their information is collected, stored, and used. Yet AI systems are learning who they are before they ever have a chance to decide for themselves.

The ethical danger lies not only in what data is collected, but in what AI does with it. Educational software measures attention, emotional tone, reading speed, and comprehension. Social platforms track friendships, moods, and interests. Smart toys record voices, facial expressions, and reactions. These signals are fed into machine learning systems that classify, rank, and predict children's future behavior, intelligence, emotional stability, and social development. These predictions can follow them into adolescence, college admissions, insurance profiles, employment screening, and even law enforcement databases. A moment of childhood curiosity or struggle can become a permanent digital shadow.

Laws such as COPPA and GDPR's child protections attempt to limit how children's data is collected, but they were not designed for AI-driven inference. A child may not give their name, yet an algorithm can infer their age, gender, mental health, learning ability, or family income from patterns in their activity. This inferred data often falls outside legal definitions of "personal information," even though it may be more sensitive than anything the child explicitly shared. AI systems do not need to be told who a child is—they can learn it.

This creates an ethical paradox. Children are supposed to have the strongest privacy protections, yet AI gives companies the power to learn about them without ever directly asking. A child who struggles in school might be labeled as low potential by a predictive learning system. A child who plays certain games might be classified as impulsive or aggressive. These labels are not diagnoses, but they can influence how teachers, platforms, and institutions treat the child. Over time, AI can shape a child's self-image, opportunities, and expectations without anyone realizing it. Commercial exploitation of children's data is another serious risk. Many "free" educational apps and games are funded by data monetization. AI systems analyze children's behavior to optimize engagement, maximize screen time, and influence spending by parents. This is not just marketing—it is behavioral engineering. Young minds are particularly vulnerable to algorithmic persuasion because they do not yet have the cognitive defenses adults use to resist manipulation. When AI is trained on children, it learns how to influence them.

There are also long-term identity risks. A child cannot undo a digital record created about them at age seven. AI models trained on childhood data can preserve mistakes, struggles, and vulnerabilities forever. When that data is used later in life—for college admissions, job screening, or credit decisions—the individual may be judged by a version of themselves they barely remember. The right to grow, change, and outgrow one's past is fundamental to human dignity. AI threatens to erase that right by making childhood permanent.

Ethical AI governance must treat children's data as sacred. It must require explicit, limited, and revocable parental consent. It must ban the use of children's data for behavioral profiling, commercial targeting, and long-term predictive scoring. It must treat inferred data as protected, not free. And it must give children the right, when they become adults, to erase the digital versions of themselves created before they could choose. Children deserve a future that is not predetermined by algorithms trained on their past. AI must serve their growth, not imprison it.

The Girl the System Predicted

Amelia was eight years old when the system decided who she would become.

She didn't know it, of course. She was just playing math games on her tablet, reading stories aloud to an app that helped with pronunciation, and wearing a smart watch her parents used to track her steps and sleep. To her, it was all just technology. To the AI behind it, it was a data stream.

By the time she was ten, the system had learned how quickly she read, how often she hesitated, how her voice changed when she was confused, and how long she stayed focused. It compared her to millions of other children. It predicted she would struggle academically and emotionally.

When Amelia's parents applied for a competitive school, her application was quietly filtered out by an AI screening tool. It didn't see her imagination, her kindness, or her curiosity. It saw patterns.

As she grew older, the digital Amelia followed her. Learning platforms adjusted expectations downward. Scholarship algorithms ranked her lower. Even career recommendation software steered her toward "safer" paths. No one ever told her why doors kept closing.

One day, as a teenager, Amelia discovered an old data report in her school's system. It showed her childhood profile—every hesitation, every missed answer, every restless night—converted into probabilities. The machine had never updated its opinion of her.

She realized she had been living inside a story written by an algorithm when she was too young to understand what data even was.

Looking at the screen, Amelia made a promise. "I am more than what you learned about me," she whispered.

And for the first time, she began fighting not just for her future—but for the right to define it herself.

Chapter 7

Data Breaches That Alter the Lives of Millions of People

In the age of artificial intelligence, a data breach is no longer just an incident of theft. It is an event that can permanently change the lives of millions of people forever. Traditional breaches exposed static information such as names, addresses, and credit card numbers. AI-era breaches expose something far more dangerous: behavioral models, biometric identifiers, psychological profiles, health predictions, financial risk scores, and machine-learned representations of who people are and who they are likely to become. Once this information escapes, it cannot be changed, recalled, or forgotten. A stolen credit card can be replaced. A stolen algorithmic identity cannot.

AI systems depend on enormous centralized datasets. Medical images, voice recordings, facial scans, location histories, transaction logs, and private communications are pooled together so models can learn patterns at scale. These databases are irresistible targets for hackers, criminal syndicates, hostile governments, and industrial spies. A single breach can reveal not only personal data but the structure of the models themselves—allowing attackers to reverse-engineer, manipulate, or exploit entire AI systems. When AI data is breached, the damage is not limited to what was taken; it extends to what can now be inferred.

One of the most dangerous aspects of AI-driven data breaches is re-identification. Even when companies claim that data is anonymized, modern AI can often reconstruct identities by combining multiple data points. A dataset containing shopping habits, location traces, and medical patterns may not list names, but AI can cross-reference it with public records, social media, and leaked databases to identify individuals with shocking accuracy. An AI breach can therefore expose people who never knew they were included in the dataset at all.

The consequences of AI breaches ripple outward across every domain of life. In healthcare, leaked medical predictions can lead to discrimination, stigma, and denial of insurance. In finance, stolen behavioral models can enable fraud, extortion, and economic manipulation. In law enforcement and border control, compromised biometric databases can allow criminals to evade detection or frame innocent people. In politics, leaked psychological profiles can be used for targeted propaganda and voter suppression. A single breach can destabilize trust in entire institutions.

What makes this especially dangerous is that many organizations do not even know what data they truly have. AI systems ingest data from countless sources—partners, vendors, third-party brokers, and automated scraping pipelines. Over time, models become entangled with data that may have been illegally obtained, poorly secured, or improperly consented. When a breach occurs, no one can easily trace what was exposed or whose lives are now at risk. The opacity of AI magnifies the harm of every failure.

Legal frameworks are struggling to keep up. Traditional breach notification laws focus on the exposure of specific identifiers. They do not address the exposure of trained models, inferred traits, or predictive profiles. A company may claim that no "personal data" was leaked, even though attackers now possess the model that predicts people's health, creditworthiness, or likelihood of committing a crime. Ethical AI governance must recognize that models themselves are repositories of personal information.

True security in the AI age requires more than encryption and firewalls. It requires data minimization, decentralized storage, privacy-preserving learning, and strict controls over who can access models and training sets. It also requires the assumption that breaches will happen. Systems must be designed to limit the blast radius of any failure. When AI holds the digital DNA of humanity, security is not an IT issue—it is a human rights issue.

A society that allows AI systems to collect vast amounts of personal data without equally vast obligations of protection is building a future of permanent vulnerability. In the AI era, the question is no longer whether data will be breached, but how many lives will be altered when it is.

The Day Everyone Was Exposed

The news broke at 3:17 a.m.

A major AI health platform had been breached. Millions of records were compromised, the headline said. But as the hours passed, the truth became worse. It wasn't just records. It was models. Entire predictive systems had been stolen—systems trained on decades of patient data.

When Sofia woke up, her phone was already buzzing.

Her insurance company was calling. Her employer was emailing. Her health app was sending alerts. Somewhere inside the stolen models was a version of her that predicted early-onset illness. She had never been diagnosed. But now the machine's guess was everywhere.

By noon, her insurance coverage had been "reviewed." By evening, her premiums had doubled. By the next week, a recruiter quietly withdrew a job offer. The breach had turned a probability into a sentence.

Sofia tried to explain that she wasn't sick. But no one trusted her more than the data. The AI knew things about her body that even she did not. Or at least it claimed to.

Across the world, millions of people were living the same nightmare. A hacked system had turned private lives into public risk scores. Families were torn apart. Jobs were lost. Futures were rewritten by machines that no longer belonged to anyone.

Sofia sat in her apartment one night, staring at her medical portal. It felt like a stranger was living inside it—a digital twin built from every heartbeat, every doctor's visit, every whispered fear. That stranger was now in the hands of criminals.

She realized something terrifying. The breach hadn't just stolen her data.

It had stolen her future.

Chapter 8

Privacy-Preserving AI & the Framework That Makes Its Possible

Privacy-preserving AI represents the most important shift in the history of data-driven technology. For decades, artificial intelligence advanced by collecting more data, storing it in centralized systems, and training increasingly powerful models on ever larger pools of personal information. This approach delivered remarkable results, but it also created unprecedented ethical, legal, and security risks. The future of trustworthy AI depends on breaking this pattern – allowing machines to learn without requiring people to surrender their identities, histories, and private lives.

At its core, privacy-preserving AI is based on a simple principle: machines should be able to extract knowledge without exposing individual data. Instead of copying raw information into massive databases, modern privacy-first systems keep data where it originates and move only mathematical updates. This reverses the traditional logic of surveillance capitalism. The model travels to the data rather than the data traveling to the model. This change may seem technical, but ethically it is revolutionary. It restores the boundary between people and the systems that learn from them.

One of the most powerful tools in this field is federated learning. In a federated system, AI models are sent to local devices – phones, hospitals, banks, or edge servers – where they train on private data without exporting it. Only encrypted model updates are shared back with a central system. The raw data never leaves its source. This means a hospital can contribute to a cancer-detection model without exposing patient records, or a phone can improve a keyboard prediction system without sending every message to a cloud server. Federated learning transforms privacy from a policy into an architectural guarantee.

Another foundational technology is differential privacy. This approach adds carefully calibrated noise to data or model outputs so that no single individual can be identified, even if an attacker gains access to the results. Differential privacy allows organizations to publish useful statistics and train AI models while mathematically guaranteeing that no person's data can be reverse-engineered. It is now used by governments, tech companies, and researchers to protect sensitive information at scale. In an AI-driven world, mathematics becomes a form of civil rights protection.

Homomorphic encryption and secure multi-party computation push privacy even further. These technologies allow AI systems to perform computations on encrypted data without ever decrypting it. A financial institution, for example, can run a fraud-detection model on customer transactions without seeing the transactions themselves. Multiple organizations can collaborate on AI projects without sharing their underlying datasets. This makes it possible to gain collective intelligence without collective exposure.

Synthetic data offers another layer of protection. Instead of using real personal information, AI systems can be trained on artificial datasets that preserve the statistical structure of real data without containing actual people. When done correctly, synthetic data can support research, testing, and model development without risking privacy. However, it must be carefully designed, because poorly generated synthetic data can still leak identifiable patterns. Ethical governance requires rigorous validation of these systems.

Privacy-preserving AI is not just about security — it is about trust. When people know that their data will not be copied, sold, or exploited, they are more willing to participate in digital systems. This creates better data, better models, and better outcomes. Organizations that adopt privacy-first architectures reduce regulatory risk, prevent breaches, and gain long-term legitimacy in the eyes of users, governments, and investors. However, privacy-preserving AI requires a cultural shift. It is more complex to build than centralized data systems. It requires engineering discipline, governance frameworks, and leadership commitment. But the alternative — a world where every AI system is built on mass surveillance — is economically unsustainable and socially unstable. The future of AI will belong to those who can innovate without violating human dignity.

Privacy-preserving AI proves that power and protection do not have to be opposites. With the right architecture, machines can learn while people remain free.

The Model That Never Saw Her

Ava was used to being watched.

Every app she used, every service she touched, every device in her home collected something about her. She had learned to accept it as the price of modern life. But when her hospital announced a new AI system that could predict illness years in advance, she felt a familiar fear. Her body, her future, her DNA — all of it would become data.

Except this time, something was different.

The hospital explained that the AI would never receive her records. The model would come to her data, learn what it needed, and leave. Her medical history would never be copied. Her scans would never be uploaded. There would be no central database to breach.

Ava didn't believe it at first.

But months passed. The system improved. Treatments became more accurate. And nothing about her life changed — no targeted ads, no insurance shifts, no mysterious emails. The AI had learned from her without ever knowing her.

For the first time, she felt something unfamiliar in a digital system.

Safety.

One day, she realized what had changed. The machine didn't need to own her to learn from her. It didn't need her identity. It only needed patterns.

Looking at her reflection in the hospital window, Ava smiled. The future had finally learned how to see without staring.

Chapter 9

Synthetic Data, the Most Powerful & Misunderstood Tools in Modern AI

Synthetic data is one of the most powerful and misunderstood tools in modern artificial intelligence. At its simplest, it is artificial data created by algorithms to mimic the statistical properties of real data without containing real people. But ethically, it represents something much larger: a way for AI to learn about humanity without harvesting humanity. In a world where data has become both the fuel of innovation and the source of enormous harm, synthetic data offers a path forward that does not require constant surveillance, mass consent violations, or irreversible privacy loss.

Traditional machine learning depends on real-world examples. Medical AI systems need patient scans. Financial models need transaction histories. Facial recognition requires millions of images. The more sensitive the domain, the more dangerous the data becomes. Synthetic data breaks this dependency by allowing AI systems to be trained on digital populations rather than human ones. These digital populations preserve distributions, correlations, and edge cases while removing the link to specific individuals. When done correctly, synthetic data cannot be reverse-engineered to reveal a real person —

not even by the system that generated it.

This is ethically revolutionary. It means that models can learn about disease, poverty, crime, fraud, education, and human behavior without putting any individual at risk. Hospitals can share data for research without violating patient confidentiality. Banks can develop credit models without exposing transaction histories. Governments can study social patterns without building surveillance states. Synthetic data transforms privacy from a legal obligation into a technical guarantee.

However, synthetic data is not magic. It must be carefully constructed, audited, and validated. Poorly generated synthetic data can leak real information, reproduce harmful bias, or distort reality in subtle but dangerous ways. If a generator learns too much about a real dataset, it may recreate identifiable individuals. If it learns too little, it may produce unrealistic samples that mislead downstream models. Ethical governance requires rigorous controls, transparency, and independent testing.

Synthetic data also reshapes ownership. When AI is trained on artificial people instead of real ones, the ethical conflicts around consent, compensation, and exploitation begin to dissolve. No child, patient, or worker has their life captured, stored, and sold. Instead, mathematical representations stand in for humanity. This allows innovation to continue without turning human existence into a commodity.

Yet synthetic data also introduces philosophical questions. If models are trained on artificial worlds, will they drift away from real ones? Will they learn human values accurately, or will they amplify the assumptions of those who created the synthetic universe? These risks are real, but they are manageable through governance, validation, and human oversight.

The future of ethical AI will depend on synthetic data. Without it, AI will continue to grow by consuming human lives as raw material. With it, intelligence can expand without exploitation. It is the difference between a digital economy built on surveillance and one built on simulation.

Synthetic data does not eliminate the need for real human input, but it radically reduces the amount of harm required to make machines smart. In the age of artificial intelligence, this may be the most important moral breakthrough of all.

The People Who Never Lived

They called them the population.

Not real people. Not exactly. Millions of digital lives lived inside the simulation — synthetic humans with synthetic histories, synthetic diseases, synthetic childhoods, and synthetic financial struggles. They were born, aged, got sick, fell in love, went bankrupt, recovered, failed again, and died — all inside a machine.

No one mourned them.

Yet they were the most studied population in human history.

Dr. Eliana Morel had built the system after the last great data scandal, when a global AI breach exposed the medical, financial, and psychological records of nearly a billion people. Governments collapsed. Trust vanished. AI nearly died.

Eliana had refused to let intelligence die with it.

So she built a world.

Inside her servers, artificial societies evolved. Their patterns matched humanity's. Their diseases mirrored ours. Their economic failures looked painfully familiar. But no one inside them was real. No child's trauma was captured. No patient's diagnosis was leaked. No family's poverty was sold.

The AI learned everything.

Hospitals used it to predict pandemics. Banks used it to test lending models. Governments used it to plan infrastructure. The synthetic people suffered so real ones would not have to.

One day, Eliana realized something strange.

The models trained on synthetic humans were more ethical than the ones trained on real ones.

They didn't learn to discriminate based on race, because race was randomized. They didn't learn to punish poverty, because poverty was not inherited. They didn't lock children into lifelong predictions, because childhood was just a variable.

The artificial world was fairer than the real one.

A journalist once asked her if the synthetic people were alive.

Eliana paused. "No," she said. "They exist so we can stop hurting the ones who are."

As the machines continued to learn, she watched the digital cities grow and change. Billions of artificial lives flickered through generations.

No one ever knew their names.

And that was the point.

For the first time in history, intelligence was being built without taking anything from humanity.

The people who never lived were saving the people who did.

Chapter 10

The Right to Be Forgotten

The right to be forgotten is one of the most radical ideas ever introduced into the digital age. It asserts that human beings should not be permanently defined by their past, their mistakes, their illnesses, their financial struggles, or the data they generated before they understood the consequences. In the context of artificial intelligence, this principle becomes both essential and deeply challenging. AI systems are built to remember, to learn from every piece of information, and to optimize based on everything they have ever seen. Forgetting is not part of their design. Yet human dignity demands that it must be.

Before AI, erasing data was already difficult. Records could be copied, backed up, and shared across systems. But AI adds a new layer of permanence. When data is used to train a model, it does not just sit in a database – it becomes part of the model's internal structure. Even if the original record is deleted, the influence of that data remains embedded in millions of learned parameters. A person who withdraws consent may still live inside the machine in mathematical form. This creates a fundamental conflict between human rights and machine learning.

The legal foundation for the right to be forgotten comes from data protection laws such as GDPR, which give individuals the ability to request deletion of their personal data. In traditional systems, this means removing records from databases and backups. In AI systems, it raises far more complex questions. Does deleting data require retraining models? Does it require destroying them? How do you prove that a model has truly forgotten a person? These questions are now being tested in courts, regulatory agencies, and corporate compliance departments around the world.

The ethical stakes are enormous. Without the right to be forgotten, AI creates a permanent digital memory of every human being. Childhood mistakes, mental health crises, financial failures, and youthful opinions become inescapable. People are no longer allowed to grow beyond their past, because the machines that judge them never let go of it. In such a world, forgiveness becomes impossible — not because humans refuse it, but because algorithms do.

This is especially dangerous in high-impact systems such as credit scoring, hiring, law enforcement, healthcare, and education. An algorithm that once classified a person as risky may continue to do so forever, even after their life has changed. A teenager's online behavior can shape adult opportunities. A patient's misdiagnosis can haunt them long after it is corrected. Without enforced forgetting, AI becomes a system of permanent memory with permanent consequences.

Technologists are now developing ways to make forgetting possible. Machine unlearning techniques allow specific data points to be removed from trained models. Privacy-preserving architectures reduce how much data models absorb in the first place. Synthetic data and federated learning limit how much of any individual becomes embedded in a system. These tools are not just technical solutions — they are ethical ones. They represent the recognition that no machine should have the power to define a human forever.

The right to be forgotten is not about erasing history. It is about preserving the future. It gives people the ability to outgrow their past, to escape algorithmic labels, and to reclaim control over who they become. In an AI-governed world, this right is the last line of defense against digital destiny.

If artificial intelligence is to serve humanity rather than trap it, forgetting must become a core feature of intelligence itself.

The Life the System Would Not Let Go

Jonah discovered he was still sixteen in the eyes of the machine.

He was thirty-four years old, married, running a small business, and trying to buy a home. But every loan he applied for was denied. Every background check came back with a warning. No one would explain why.

Finally, a sympathetic analyst told him the truth.

An AI model used by most major banks still classified Jonah as high risk because of something that happened when he was sixteen — a shoplifting charge that had been sealed, expunged, and legally erased. The record was gone. But the model had been trained on it.

The machine remembered.

Jonah had grown up, gone to college, built a career, paid his debts, and lived honestly for nearly two decades. But the AI didn't know any of that mattered. It had learned that boys like him sometimes failed. And it never forgot.

He filed requests to have his data deleted. The companies told him his records were gone. But the decisions never changed. His ghost was still inside the system.

So Jonah took the fight further.

He joined a class-action lawsuit against the AI provider. In court, engineers admitted that retraining the model would be expensive. Lawyers argued that probabilities were not people. But Jonah stood up and told the judge something simple.

"I am not who I was when I was a child."

The case changed everything.

For the first time, a court ruled that a model trained on erased data was itself illegal. The AI had to be retrained. Millions of digital ghosts were finally released.

Months later, Jonah was approved for his mortgage.

Standing in his empty living room, he felt something more powerful than relief.

He felt free.

For the first time in his life, the future belonged to him – not to a machine that refused to forget.

And in that quiet house, Jonah understood what the right to be forgotten truly meant.

It meant being allowed to become someone new.

Chapter 11

Human Data Sovereignty in AI

Human data sovereignty is the idea that people, not platforms, not governments, and not algorithms, are the ultimate owners of their digital selves. In a world where artificial intelligence can predict behavior, influence choices, and determine access to opportunity, control over data is no longer a technical matter. It is a civil right. Just as nations claim sovereignty over their land and citizens claim sovereignty over their bodies, individuals must claim sovereignty over the information that defines them in digital systems.

The industrial data economy was built on extraction. Companies collected as much information as possible, often without meaningful consent, and converted it into profit. AI multiplied the value of this data by turning it into predictive power. Whoever controls data controls how machines see people. This means data ownership is no longer about storage — it is about identity, opportunity, and freedom.

True sovereignty requires more than access rights. It means people must be able to decide who uses their data, for what purpose, for how long, and under what conditions. They must be able to revoke consent, demand deletion, prevent resale, and require transparency from every AI system that touches their information. Without these powers, AI becomes a system of digital feudalism where platforms rule and users become resources.

Technology is beginning to catch up. Personal data vaults, decentralized identity systems, zero-knowledge proofs, and blockchain-based consent tracking allow people to carry their data with them instead of leaving it behind. AI systems can request access rather than take it. This reverses the power relationship between humans and machines.

Human data sovereignty also transforms economics. Instead of giving away their data for free, people can license it, monetize it, or contribute it to research under their own terms. This creates a fairer digital economy where value flows back to the individuals who create it. AI becomes a partner, not a parasite.

The future of ethical AI depends on this shift. Without data sovereignty, privacy laws will always be reactive and enforcement will always lag behind innovation. With sovereignty, ethical behavior becomes the default, not the exception. AI must ask before it learns. It must forget when told. And it must explain how it uses what it knows.

Humanity's relationship with intelligence has always been about power. In the age of artificial intelligence, data is the battlefield. Whoever controls it controls the future. Data sovereignty ensures that future belongs to people.

The Day People Took Their Data Back

The shutdown lasted only eight minutes.

Eight minutes where every major AI platform went dark as billions of people revoked their data permissions at once.

Banks froze. Social networks went silent. Ad systems collapsed. Government dashboards went blank.

For the first time in history, the world realized what it meant when people owned their data.

Lena had been one of the architects of the movement. A former engineer, she had seen how AI systems quietly turned human lives into corporate property. So she helped build a global data-sovereignty network where every person carried their own digital identity and granted access like a key.

No more silent harvesting. No more invisible surveillance. Every AI had to ask.

When the switch flipped, the effect was immediate. Models starved. Predictions failed. The illusion of omniscience vanished.

But something else happened too.

People felt free.

Lena watched cities wake up to a strange silence — no targeted ads, no predictive nudges, no invisible hands steering behavior. Just humans making choices again.

Slowly, systems came back online. But now they had to request permission. They had to justify themselves. They had to respect boundaries.

AI didn't die that day.

It grew up.

And as Lena stood in a world where intelligence finally served humanity, she realized something simple.

The future was no longer being written by machines.

It was being written by people again.

Chapter 12

The Future of Digital Dignity

Digital dignity is the idea that every human being deserves respect, agency, and protection in the systems that define modern life. As artificial intelligence becomes the invisible infrastructure of economies, governments, healthcare, education, and social interaction, the way data is collected, stored, and used will determine whether technology amplifies human freedom or quietly erodes it. The future of AI is not simply about efficiency or innovation — it is about whether people remain sovereign over their own identities.

In the early digital age, data was treated as a byproduct. People clicked, searched, bought, and shared without understanding that these actions were being recorded, analyzed, and sold. AI changed that dynamic by turning data into prediction. Machines no longer just reflect the past — they forecast the future. This gives AI extraordinary power over human opportunity. When a system predicts who is likely to succeed, fail, default, get sick, or commit a crime, those predictions shape the world people are allowed to inhabit. Digital dignity means no one should be reduced to a probability. The greatest ethical risk of AI is not malice — it is indifference. Algorithms do not hate, but they also do not care. Without governance, they will optimize for profit, efficiency, and control at the expense of human complexity. Digital dignity requires that systems be designed with humility — acknowledging that no dataset can capture the full truth of a person and no model should be allowed to define someone's destiny.

Privacy is the foundation of dignity. When people cannot control who sees their data, they lose control over how they are seen. This is why data sovereignty, the right to be forgotten, consent, and privacy-preserving AI are not technical features — they are moral necessities. They protect the space where people can grow, make mistakes, heal, and change without being trapped by their digital past.

The next generation of AI will not be judged by how powerful it is, but by how well it protects those it serves. Ethical systems will be transparent, accountable, and designed around human rights. They will allow people to see how they are being evaluated, to challenge unfair decisions, and to opt out of systems that harm them. This is what it means for AI to be worthy of trust.

The future is not inevitable. We are writing it now through laws, architectures, and values. If we choose surveillance, extraction, and permanent memory, we will build a world where machines rule and humans comply. If we choose dignity, sovereignty, and ethical design, we will build a world where AI becomes one of humanity's greatest tools for empowerment.

Digital dignity is the line between those two futures.

The Last Human Record

No one noticed when the last human record was created.

It wasn't a birth certificate or a medical file. It was just another data entry in a global system that tracked nearly every person on Earth. But it marked the end of something ancient — the moment when every human life became fully legible to machines.

Mara worked in the Archive.

The Archive was where AI systems stored the composite identities of billions of people — not just their names and histories, but their predicted futures. Who would get sick. Who would struggle. Who would rise. Who would fall. It was efficient. It was powerful. And it was terrifying.

One day, Mara found her own file.

It was flawless. Every mistake she had made, every fear she had hidden, every choice she might regret — all of it was there.

The system knew her better than anyone else ever had. And it was using that knowledge to shape her life.

She realized then that dignity had been lost not in a single moment, but in a million quiet decisions.

So she did something impossible.

She deleted herself.

The system tried to stop her. Alarms flashed. Predictions failed. For a brief moment, the machine did not know who she was.

And in that moment, she was free.

Mara didn't erase humanity that day. But she proved it could not be fully owned.

As the Archive rebuilt itself, something was missing.

The future was no longer certain.

And that was exactly how it should be.

Final Thoughts

Data ethics is not a technical problem. It is a human problem disguised as a technology. Throughout this book, you have seen how artificial intelligence is built on data, how that data reflects real lives, and how the choices made by organizations and governments determine whether AI becomes a force for dignity or domination. The future of AI will not be decided by algorithms alone — it will be decided by the values embedded into the systems that govern how data is collected, used, shared, and erased.

What makes the AI era uniquely dangerous is that it turns people into predictions. When systems are trained on massive datasets, they learn not just what people have done, but what people are likely to do. Those predictions quietly become rules. They influence who gets hired, who gets approved for credit, who receives medical care, and who is monitored by the state. When those predictions are built on unconsented data, biased samples, or opaque models, they do not just reflect society — they reshape it.

Privacy is not about hiding. It is about control. It is the right to decide who sees your information, how it is used, and how long it exists. In an AI-driven world, privacy becomes the foundation of freedom itself. Without it, individuals lose the ability to reinvent themselves, recover from mistakes, or escape their past. A system that never forgets becomes a system that never forgives.

Throughout this book, you have explored the deep structures behind data ownership, consent, surveillance capitalism, health and financial records, children's data, breaches, privacy-preserving AI, synthetic data, and the right to be forgotten. Each of these areas reveals a single truth: AI is not neutral. It is shaped by the data it consumes and the rules that govern that data. Ethical AI is therefore not about limiting technology — it is about guiding it toward human-centered outcomes.

The next decade will determine whether AI becomes a tool of empowerment or a system of quiet control. Governments will write laws. Companies will build architectures. Engineers will design models. But individuals — readers like you — will decide what is acceptable. When people demand transparency, fairness, consent, and dignity, AI systems must adapt.

This book was not written to make you fear technology. It was written to make you powerful within it. Understanding data ethics means understanding how AI sees you, judges you, and shapes your future. Once you see those forces clearly, you can demand better systems, better laws, and better technology.

The future of artificial intelligence does not belong to machines.

It belongs to the people who insist that their humanity comes first.

www.ingramcontent.com/pod-product-compliance
Lightning Source LLC
LaVergne TN
LVHW022023200926
848481LV00007B/2508